# The Writer's Eye 2002

*An anthology of poetry and prose
by the winners of the
16th annual literary competition*

Rosemarie Koch, Chair
Janis Chevalier, Co-Chair
Jane Williamson, Co-Chair

**University of Virginia Art Museum**
Charlottesville, Virginia

*Past Judges of High School and Adult Divisions*

| | |
|---|---|
| 1988 | Charles Wright |
| 1989 | Sheila McMillen and Debra Nystrom |
| 1990 | John Casey and Michael Ryan |
| 1991 | Judy Longley and Mary Lee Settle |
| 1992 | Sydney Blair and Rita Dove |
| 1993 | George Garrett and Lisa Spaar |
| 1994 | Douglas Day and Gregory Orr |
| 1995 | Rita Mae Brown and Stephen Cushman |
| 1996 Spring | Karl D. Ackerman |
| 1996 Fall | David Maurer and Charles Wright |
| 1997 | John Grisham and Gregory Orr |
| 1998 | Jonathan Coleman and Tan A. Lin |
| 1999 | Avery Chenoweth and George Garrett |
| 2000 | Karl Ackerman and Jerome McGann |
| 2001 | Debra Nystrom and Christopher Tilghman |

ISBN 1-57427-143-1
Copyright © 2002
The Rector and Visitors
of the University of Virginia

Design by Carolyn Weary Brandt

Library of Congress Control Number: 2003100424

**Howell Press, Inc.**
1713-2D Allied Lane
Charlottesville, VA 22903
(434) 977-4006
www.howellpress.com

**Cover image:**
Thomas Moran (American, 1837-1926)
*On the Catawissa Creek, 1862*
Oil on canvas, 14 x 20¼ inches
Gift of Gil Michaels, 2002.5

# The Writer's Eye 2002
## University of Virginia Art Museum

*The Writer's Eye*, now in its sixteenth year, is an annual literary competition organized by the docents of the University of Virginia Art Museum. The competition invites people to unite the verbal with the visual by giving writers an opportunity to create original poetry and prose inspired by works of art in the Museum. Contestants submit entries in four categories: grades 3-5, 6-8, 9-12 and University/ Adult. Judges for grades 3-8 entries are writers, English teachers from local schools and University of Virginia faculty and staff. Professional writers judge all High School and University/Adult entries. An awards ceremony in February recognizes the winners.

To help the aspiring writers, docent-led tours are designed to explore the connections between the ways artists and writers express their ideas, values and observations of our world. Inquiry-based tours strive to stimulate imagination and creativity and use provocative questions to enable the visitor to discover and translate the language of art into written words. A variety of activities within the tours, such as role-playing, writing of cinquains and acrostics, drawing, screen and play writing are designed to highlight thematic and other aspects of the artworks that may offer inspiration to participants. Packets containing color reproductions of the images, as well as a fully illustrated web site, are also available to entrants.

Last year, the docents gave approximately 155 *Writer's Eye* tours to more than 1,500 people, including students of all ages from public and private schools in Charlottesville and Albemarle County, as well as Orange, Madison, Afton, Stuarts Draft and Staunton, Virginia. This year, the Museum received a record number of entries—more than 1,200. Even for those who choose not to enter the competition, the *Writer's Eye* offers a wonderful opportunity to explore the connections between art and literature, artist and writer.

# Table of Contents

# Award Winners

## Elementary (Grades 3-5)

**Poetry**

| | | |
|---|---|---|
| First | Sarah Mary Goldfarb | Walker Upper |
| Second | Emily Moffett | Brownsville |
| Third | Zoë Ackerman | Village |
| | Candice Roland | Virginia L. Murray |
| *Honorable Mention* | | |
| | Kristen Bicknell | Cale |

**Prose**

| | | |
|---|---|---|
| First | Emily Berg | Meriwether Lewis |
| Second | Joshua Scharf | Venable |
| Third | Neil Branch | Virginia L. Murray |
| *Honorable Mention* | | |
| | Virginia Mead | Virginia L. Murray |
| | Linge Sun | Greer |
| | Leah Catherine Kessenich | Nathanael Greene |

## Middle School (Grades 6-8)

**Poetry**

| | | |
|---|---|---|
| First | Natalie Goldfarb | Buford |
| Second | Josephine Blount | Tandem |
| Third | Paul Michel | Jackson P. Burley |
| *Honorable Mention* | | |
| | Molly Marx | J.T. Henley |

**Prose**

| | | |
|---|---|---|
| First | Dakota Cox | Grymes Memorial |
| Second | William Gillespie | Jackson P. Burley |
| Third | Beth Foster | Jack Jouett |
| *Honorable Mention* | | |
| | Garner Takahashi-Morris | Buford |
| | Kaitlyn Potter | Walton |

## High School (Grades 9-12)

**Poetry**

| | | |
|---|---|---|
| First | Claire Whitenack | Albemarle |
| Second | Jocelyn Spaar | Charlottesville |
| Third | Meg Lally | Charlottesville |
| *Honorable Mention* | | |
| | Alex Chase-Levenson | Charlottesville |
| | Avery Lawrence | Charlottesville |
| | Jameson Zimmer | Renaissance |

**Prose**
First                    Thomas Moruza              Charlottesville
Second                Stefan Hench                Charlottesville
Third                    Alison Kilian               Charlottesville
*Honorable Mention*

                                Lauren E. Walker       Homeschooled, ACTS
                                Emily Quanbeck        Charlottesville
                                Keith Groomes         Charlottesville

### University/Adult

**Poetry**
First                    Don Whitenack
Second                Catherine W. Glover
Third                    James Nohrnberg

**Prose**
First                    Jennifer Whitenack
Second                Adrienne So
Third                    Marjorie W. Shepherd
*Honorable Mention*

                                  Anya Johnson
                                Karen J. Ratzlaff
                                Stephen Keach

# Acknowledgments

Taking over an interesting and comprehensive project like this year's 16th annual *Writer's Eye Poetry and Prose Competition* was an honor as well as a challenge for me. It could only succeed with the support of many dedicated people who contributed their time and knowledge toward the success of this endeavor. A special thank you is going to Janis Chevalier who willingly provided her expertise and joined in all the many tasks to accomplish this venture. I also thank Jane Williamson, whose contributions were invaluable.

The following professionals were not only dedicated but enthusiastic in performing their duties as judges, most of them for many years. Together they read and judged more than 1,200 entries. My heartfelt thanks to each of them for their contribution.

**Elementary School**
(grades 3, 4, 5) judges
Roberta Platts-Mills
Beverly Van Hook
Susan Washko
Nura Yingling

**Middle School**
(grades 6, 7, 8) judges
Heather Burns
Mark Collins
Suzanne Freeman
Wendy Gavin
Michele Kellermann
P. Parke Muth

**High School** (grades 9, 10, 11, 12) and **University/Adult** judges

Susan Tyler Hitchcock, prose judge, is the author of six books, among them *Gather Ye Wild Things: A Forager's Year* (1980) and her family sailing memoir *Coming About: A Family Passage at Sea* (1998). Locally, she is known for her essays in the magazine *Albemarle* and her radio commentaries on WINA.

Stephen Cushman, poetry judge, teaches at the University of Virginia, where he is Robert C. Taylor Professor of English and director of the International Center for American Studies. He also is the author of five books, including the nonfiction work *Bloody Pajamas* (1998) and *Cussing Lesson* (2002).

Without the volunteer docents of the University of Virginia Art Museum who contributed hundreds of hours of their time by giving 139 tours to 1,439 students and helping with numerous administrative details this *Writer's Eye* would not have happened. Many thanks to each and every one of them.

Last but not least, I want to thank the entire University of Virginia Art Museum staff. Jill Hartz, Michael Alexander, Jean Collier, Suzanne Foley, Stephen Margulies, Rusty Smith, as well as Jane Anne Young and Kimberly Lytle, provided much-appreciated support and encouragement in a variety of ways.

And finally many thanks go to the following organizations for their generous funding and continuing support of the *Writer's Eye Poetry and Prose Competition:*

**BARNES&NOBLE**
BOOKSELLERS

Bizou
Blue Whale Books
Carmello's
College Inn
Escafé
Hamilton's
Heartwood Books
Howell Press

LexisNexis
Maharaja Indian Cuisine
Metro
Mono Loco Restaurant
New Dominion Book Shop
Northern Exposure Restaurant
Rapture
Sweetbones
Station
University of Virginia Bookstore

Rosemarie Koch, *Writer's Eye* Chair, 2002

# Introduction

For 16 years, a variety of art has been selected at the University of Virginia Art Museum to serve as the inspiration for aspiring writers from third grade through University/Adult. This year, the imagination of more than 1,200 individuals was stirred and resulted in prose and poetry entries that bring the richness of language to the experience of visual art. We do not know how art began any more than we know how language started, but in these winning entries they both come together and form a wonderful unity.

*Great prose writing—probably all good writing, no matter what genre—succeeds through a balance between ingenuity and formality.*

*Ingenuity gives a piece of writing its design, its point, its purpose. It is the new and different idea that drives the writing. A piece's governing idea should be interesting, intriguing, slightly mystifying, and ultimately satisfying.*

*Formality in writing means respecting the rules of the written language: writing without any unplanned misspellings, bad grammar, punctuation oddities. Great writing can sound conversational; to have formality, it need not be stuffy.*

*Great writing glides into the reader's brain without bumps or hesitations or loopbacks to figure out meaning. Formality in writing lets the ingenuity shine through.*

**Susan Tyler Hitchcock,**
Prose Judge 2002 for the
University/Adult categories

*Poems are like people. There are very few everybody likes and very few nobody likes. Like a person, a poem has many ways to be winning, attractive, charming, likable, and this short statement can't possibly inventory them all. That said, here are the things I found myself looking for.*

*The sound. Whatever else they are, however else they may be likable, the best poems are also distinct shapes made of sound. They don't have to have meter; they don't have to rhyme. But they do have to live fully in the mind's ear, and they do so by establishing some kind of memorable, compelling rhythm.*

*Avoidance of vague, tired, overly familiar, poetic-sounding thought and language. Too often when people start to write poems, they abandon the rich pungency of the language they actually speak and lapse into the stiff, stilted language of what they think of as how a poem should sound.*

*Degree of difficulty. At some level a good haiku isn't as impressive as a poem that's more ambitious in what it tries to do, either formally or tonally or conceptually or figuratively, even if it doesn't quite pull it off.*

*Unwavering focus. It's not hard to tell when, after several good lines or stanzas, the mind behind the poem began to wander. Imagination and creativity and daring leaps of association are often welcome, but they differ from faltering attention in what they produce.*

*Personality, freshness, originality. We treasure these qualities in people. How can we not want them in poems?*

**Stephen Cushman,**
Poetry Judge 2002 for the
University/Adult categories

# Art Selected for the Competition

Tiziano Aspetti (Italian, 1565-1607)
*Vulcan*, ca. 1590
Bronze on wood base, 24 inches high
Gift of the Society of Benefactors and Patrons, 1985.41

Francesco Caucig (Austro-Hungarian, 1755-1828)
*Queen Esther Before King Ahasuerus*, ca. 1815
Oil on canvas, $55^{3}/_{4}$ x $81^{1}/_{2}$ inches
Museum Purchase, 1976.19

John P. Stewart (American, born 1945)
*The Age of Fire and Ice*, 1975
Acrylic on canvas, 72 x 61 inches
Paul Goodloe McIntire Fund Purchase, 1975.31

Roy De Forest (American, born 1930)
*The American Cowboy*, 1976
Colored pencil, graphite and pastel on paper, $22^{1}/_{2}$ x 30 inches
Museum Purchase, 1976.14

Eugène Delacroix (French, 1798-1863)
*Lion Devouring a Horse (Lion devorant un cheval)*, 1844
Lithograph, $6^{3}/_{4}$ x $9^{1}/_{4}$ inches (image)
Museum Purchase with Curriculum Support Funds, 1996.25.1

Kai Ch'i (1773-1828)
Chinese, Ch'ing dynasty,1644-1911
*Lady in Her Study with Attendants*, 1821
Hanging scroll, ink and color on paper, 38 x 17 inches
Collection of the University of Michigan Museum of Art. On view in *The Orchid
Pavilion Gathering: Chinese Paintings from the University of Michigan Art Museum*

Käthe Kollwitz (German, 1867-1945)
*Working Woman in Profile Facing Left (Arbeiterfrau im Profil nach links)*, 1903
Lithograph on Japanese paper, $16^{7}/_{8}$ x $11^{7}/_{8}$ inches (image)
Museum Purchase with Curriculum Support Funds, 1997.6.2

Raymond Parker (American, 1922-1990)
*Untitled*, 1960
Oil on canvas, $80^{3}/_{4}$ x $69^{7}/_{8}$ inches
Presented by Samuel M. Kootz, L.L.B. 1921, in memory of William C. Seitz (1914-
1974), William R. Kenan, Jr., Professor of Art History, 1970-1974, 1975.1

Lang-Shih-ning/Giuseppe Castiglione (Italian, 1688-1766), attributed to Chinese, Ch'ing dynasty, 1644-1911
*Bird on a Bamboo Branch*, 1688-1766
Folding fan on paper with an ink and color painting on one side and a long poem in ink on the verso, 14⁷/₈ x 24¹/₄ inches
Collection of the University of Michigan Museum of Art.
On view in *The Orchid Pavilion Gathering: Chinese Paintings from the University of Michigan Art Museum*

Charles Meryon (French, 1821-1868)
*Le Pont-au-Change*, 1854
Etching with drypoint, 6¹/₈ x 13³/₁₆ inches (plate)
Museum Purchase with Curriculum Support Funds, 1992.16.2

Thomas Moran (American, 1837-1926)
*On the Catawissa Creek*, 1862
Oil on canvas, 14 x 20¹/₄ inches
Gift of Gil Michaels, 2002.5

Italo Scanga (American, 1932-2001)
*Red Cube and Trees*, 1997
Painted steel, 12 x 12 x 11¹/₂ inches
Gift of the artist, 1998.3

Sheng Mao-yeh (active 1594-1640)
Chinese, Ming dynasty, 1368-1644
*The Orchid Pavilion Gathering*, 1621 (detail)
Handscroll, ink and color on silk, 12³/₈ x 86 inches
Collection of the University of Michigan Museum of Art
On view in *The Orchid Pavilion Gathering: Chinese Paintings from the University of Michigan Museum of Art*

John P. Stewart (American, born 1945)
*The Age of Fire and Ice*, 1975
Acrylic on canvas, 72 x 61 inches
Paul Goodloe McIntire Fund Purchase, 1975.31

William Wylie (American, born 1957)
*Untitled* from *Stillwater* exhibition, 2000
Gelatin silver print, 20 x 24 inches
Lent by the artist

## Works Not Illustrated

Bartolo di Fredi (Italian, ca. 1330-1410)
*Seven Saints in Adoration*, 1367
Tempera and gold leap on panel, 11⁷/₈ x 9⁷/₈ inches
Gift of Mrs. Daniel W. Evans, 1975.49.1

Benjamin West (American, 1738-1820, active in London)
*Juno Receiving the Cestus from Venus,* 1771
Oil on canvas, 90⅝ x 75⅜ inches.
Purchased with proceeds of the Benefit Auction sponsored by the Volunteer Board of
the Bayly Art Museum and other funds, 1981.19

Angelica Kauffman (Swiss, 1741-1807)
*Ulysses and Circe,* 1786
Oil on canvas, 55 x 41¼ inches
Membership Acquisition Fund Purchase, 1976.24

*Bust of a Woman*
Palmyra, 211 A.D.
Limestone, 18½ x 17 x 8 inches
Museum Purchase with Curriculum Support Funds, 2001.16.2

William Zorach (American, 1889-1966)
*The Dancer,* 1938
Bronze, 24¼ x 17 x 14 inches
Anonymous Gift in Honor of Mrs. Virginia Britton Lowthrop, 1977.8

Wu Ch'ing-yqn (?-1916)
*Autumn Moon at Mt. Tung-t'ing,* 1903
Hanging scroll, ink and light color on paper, 73 x 38½ inches
Collection of the University of Michigan Museum of Art. On view in the *The Orchid
Pavilion Gathering: Chinese Paintings from the University of Michigan Museum of Art*

Lang-Shih-ning/Giuseppe Castiglione (Italian,
1688-1766), attributed to Chinese, Ch'ing
dynasty, 1644-1911
*Bird on a Bamboo Branch*, 1688-1766
Folding fan on paper with an ink and color
painting on one side and a long poem in ink on
the verso, 14⁷/₈ x 24¹/₄ inches
Collection of the University of Michigan Museum
of Art. On view in *The Orchid Pavilion Gathering:
Chinese Paintings from the University of Michigan
Museum of Art*.

First Place, Poetry, Grades 6-8

# Bird on a Bamboo Branch

*Natalie Goldfarb*
*Buford Middle School*

Sometimes.
When all is still—
excepting breaths
not yet taken.
And rain
plinking
collecting
running down windows
like Tears.
I look in the attic.
Find magic
long
forgotten.
I open the
folds.
dust covers
the air.
Burnt sun spots
rotating
Hidden in a memory.
shimmering like
day
on the wood of
Ancestors.
ghosts of love
long
forgotten.
Emotions
colored to be
delicate
fragile.
un-noticed.
A white bird
sits.
Jabbers at blooms
delicately opening.
Words carved.
cutting thick
chunks of
my soul.
Setting them
on
paper.

First Place, Prose, Grades 6-8

# The Empress and the Fan

*Dakota Cox*
*Grymes Memorial School*

The heavily ornamented woman fans herself. A delicate white bird with a tiny blue head decorates the fan. It flits back and forth through the air on the folded paper. The scent of her mingling perfumes entices the Emperor's court. The white powder that is caked on her pale skin covers her face like a mask. The woman, Empress Lashang, watches as her husband, the newly crowned Emperor, listens with no concern for the farmers' complaints. They have just been asked to give thirty extra acres of rice to the king. The ragged lot kneels on the richly carpeted floor of the throne room. Their dusty clothing and wild eyes seem out of place against the lush surroundings. The Empress takes two steps back; her silk dress rustles as she falls into the shadow of the throne. She watches her husband motion for the guards to take the men away. Lashang's head drops as her husband once again ignores the problems of his people. The ancient farmer, with skin stained brown by hours of grueling labor under the hot sun, is dragged helplessly from the room, pleading with the Emperor until the door is slammed in his face. Visions of the ensuing horrors flash through her mind. She imagines the black cage door being shut for eternity and locked by laughing guards, the last people the hopeless man would ever see. Her sad black eyes drift across the fan, noticing the intricacy of the painting, the meticulous veining of each leaf, the tiny painted ridges of the feathers. Once again, the scene comes alive in her mind's eye.

*The white bird flies to the top of a steep cliff to drink nectar from the magical red flower that grows there.* She snaps back to reality as the Emperor laughs in the face of a man who says he does not have any rice to give. A steely determination flashes through her eyes. The Emperor must be stopped and the family heirloom, passed down through many generations, is how she would save her beloved homeland from its tyrannical leader. Her eyes leaped from her husband to the odd piece of wood on the side of her fan, which is engraved with ancient markings from a long forgotten language. She runs her fingers over the worn writing, stirring the smell of bamboo and also the memories of her mother teaching her how to read the etchings. The smell brings back the feel of her mother's soft hands as she moved her thin fingers across the ancient wood many years ago. The soothing sound of her mother's whispers in her ear as they secretly practiced reading the forbidden carvings. The Empress had picked it up with much ease: learning in two days that which had taken her mother ten years. The words came easily to her now as she began to recite the words that would rid her wonderful country of their tyrannical king. She spoke the words softly at first, but as the power began to build inside of her, she spoke the words louder and louder until she was screaming them in the face of her husband. "Yashey tu yadet ella fashney," she chanted for the final time in her husband's face. A fog began to materialize in the throne room. The tendrils slowly slithered across the floor to lap at the feet of the oversized hickory throne. The emperor was frozen within the space of a heartbeat. Everybody in the room was still, petrified by the powerful spell. The fog began to engulf the statue on its throne of stolen gold. Empress Lashang began to fan the fog away after it had swallowed her husband. Gradually, the fog melted away and a new scene appeared. There was no tyrannical king, no throne of stolen gold, and no poor farmers kneeling at an evil leader's feet to give him their last pieces of rice. Her country was saved. She stood before her people and proclaimed, "Your enemy is gone. He has been vanquished. I will take his place as Empress and you will never again see hardship."

The silken robes that hung around her in intricate folds rustled as she moved to take her place in the center of the raised dais where her husband once sat. Her black eyes were not filled with steel anymore; instead there was a willingness to rule kindly. Her attendants watched her with a new awe. She had been changed from a weak Empress to a strong-willed leader, ready to rule justly.

Empress Lashang rules her country for forty more years with love and kindness. As legend goes, a tiny white bird was often seen flitting around her head, singing songs of peace in her ear. The fan she had cherished many years ago, she discarded after she banished her husband. A maid who worked for the Empress carried it to the fire. Its flames licked around her, as she stood ready to burn the fan. On an impulse, the woman looked down at it. The white bird that once sat on a bamboo branch was no longer the center of the fan. Instead, it was perched on the shoulder of the Empress dressed in a gown of fine silk, and at her feet knelt a ragged man with the face of the old Emperor. The woman, thinking the fan to be of some value, hid the fan beneath her apron and kept it to hand down as a family heirloom until a descendant learns the secret of the fan.

**Thomas Moran (American, 1837-1926)**
*On the Catawissa Creek,* **1862**
Oil on canvas, 14 x 20$^1/_4$ inches
Gift of Gil Michaels, 2002.5

# Straining Water with a Rusty Wooden Bucket On the Catawissa Creek

*Meg Lally*
*Charlottesville High School*

Russell says the cows are kissing their other selves
That live under the water when they hunch
And slurp, but I know better.

My cotton white is spotted with happy dark spots.
As if one tree isn't beautiful
Enough. There is another just as tall
And brown, to hang from and carve in.
(Brushing knuckles over the barkish wet.)
Russell says don't fall into the puddles
When you try and look inside. But I know
Better, as I try to kiss my other self.
Wooden buckets draw sweet catches,
Sweeter than Chesapeake bug insides.
Counting moos on my sticky fingers,
Is an appropriate way to paddle away.

Russell says it's time to go, and I say
Wait until the cows make sense, and
For my days to be boring again.

**Francesco Caucig (Austro-Hungarian, 1755-1828)**
*Queen Esther Before King Ahasuerus,* ca. 1815
Oil on canvas, 55³/₄ x 81¹/₂ inches
Museum Purchase, 1976.19

# Esther Expires, Melodramatically: Audition & Reading for the Holy Day of Purim

*James Nohrnberg*

*Esther is among the Hebrew Bible's final books, and the original text never mentions God. But the rabbis say that upon the Last Day it will be the only one remaining of all the many pieces that make up the Scriptures. "La Juive" is the opera of Halèvy discussed in The Modern Library's "Metropolitan Opera Guide" (1939) in Chap. 5, "Opera Dresses Up": its story shares literary motifs with the Book of Esther (Caruso killed himself singing it).*

> The great galoot himself is much upset,
> Arousing from a bathtub throne to greet
> A reinstated bride. Thus opera dresses up.
>
> The ivory scepter leans its length of rule aside
> A peacock's siege, bone-white, not occupied
> Without its phantom limb unsteadying within.
>
> The Queen concedes her foreign stock and pedigree
> By toppling off the modest pedestal
> Which were her own two feet. No fainting-couch
>
> In sight, the maids idolatrous embrace
> Asiatic Majesty's saturated case.
> Over-scaled doll presents the bovine groan
>
> Of double bass. A-perch the throne-room's
> Upper deck, a stolid sphinx makes mock
> Of five arriving swanboats, swooning senseless
>
> At the dock. Clouds of incense, or evil genie,
> Billow off the wall: local golem's
> Anamorphic smoke, or roccoco's
>
> Empty wreath. Beneath the stall and seat
> Of Kings of Kings, pre-recording for posterity:
> An inclined stylus eye, scripting *La Juive.*
>
> Of heart devout, and hallowing a Name
> Spake never he aloud, does Xerxes' scribe divine
> Their self-eclipsing Ishtar, fallen and alone,
>
> Enscroll ere long His latest strain, and days
> His Kingdom comes, serenade the Throne,
> *Ego sum scriptura sola, sola scriptura,*
>
> Her unaccompanied coloratura?

**Eugène Delacroix (French, 1798-1863)**
*Lion Devouring a Horse (Lion devorant un cheval)*, 1844
Lithograph, 6³/₄ x 9¹/₄ inches (image)
Museum Purchase with Curriculum Support Funds, 1996.25.1

First Place, Prose, Grades 9-12

# The Scent of Fear

*Thomas Moruza*
*Charlottesville High School*

It had been hot the whole day. The sun bore down upon the masses of bustling people in the market, causing them to retire under the shade of the market-side canvases. For the old man, it was a long and tiresome day as well, and he did not look forward to traveling across the mountains that night to his home. He painstakingly packed the remainder of the thick hand-woven rugs not sold and loaded them onto his old horse, her knees buckling slightly as he pushed them onto her bony back. The mare was his companion and had always been good-tempered, despite the amount of work he demanded from her.

As he finished, he prepared himself for the dangerous passage across the mountains that he had crossed so many times. He prayed to Allah, "Lord, thou art the creator, I am only created; Thou art my sovereign, I am only thy servant; Thou art the helper, I am only the beseecher; Thou art the forgiver, I am the sinner; Thou, my Lord, art the Merciful, All-knowing, All-loving." His thoughts strayed to the fears that awaited him in the utter darkness of the mountain pass.

He then thought about his wife and children, how they were waiting upon his safe return. He smiled as he recalled the last time he had returned after a week of trading and saw his little daughter skip outside to greet him.

The old man then mounted his horse with the slowness of age and the pair moved off, melding into the crowd. By evening they reached the city limits and plodded steadily down the dirt road leading to the mountains. A troop of mounted soldiers galloped by, raising a dust cloud that left the two snorting and coughing.

The air chilled as they began to climb the steady incline of the all-but-inviting mountains. The old man gazed for a moment at the peach, red and purple hues of the Persian sunset. Regardless of the beautiful sky, the lofty pass still looked gray, bleak and threatening. Stiffly, he pulled on a woolen tunic to ward off the cold wind that rushed through the trees and assailed his face and hands. The sun was set now and moonless night descended upon the travelers.

The rocky pass loomed ahead and he could barely make out the black caves that lined the path. A long drop on either side of the approach to the pass reminded him of how carefully his mare would pick her way across it. He stopped her before the entrance and peered into the darkness. In the eerie silence the old mare began to fidget and her ears perked forward at a small sound ahead. Since the old man could only see several feet before him, it was impossible to tell what had caught her attention. Silence reigned, but she would not move forward. She sidestepped and tossed her head. The old man pried his heels into her stubborn sides, but she only grew more agitated. Her eyes and nostrils widened in panic and she hesitantly stepped backward. The old man dismounted and pressed his warm, wrinkled hand against her face to calm her. At the touch of his hand, she threw her nose high in the air and pawed the turf. The old man turned to search the pass opening and noticed something peculiar. The pass entrance had suddenly blackened, covered by a shadow. It seemed strange to him until he realized what it must be and blanched; the lions that inhabited the Persian mountains were fearsome. Large, vicious beasts, they preyed on passing travelers. He stealthily backed away a good distance, turned, and hid behind a tree. His horse still pranced a few feet ahead, too wary to turn her back and retreat. Pressing his back against the trunk, the man tried to calm himself and not think about the fate that could befall them in this delicate situation. He fervently beseeched Allah for protection.

The old man suddenly crept out across the ground on all fours to his frightened mare. He retrieved one of his rugs and approached the entrance cautiously. His hand shook in fright; he had a sudden change in mind, dropped the rug, and scuttled back to his hiding place. The sound of the heavy rug thudding on the path galvanized the beast into action. After crouching for several minutes, watching the man comfort his horse, approach him and then retreat again, it pounced. In an enormous leap, it landed on the mare's back. The weight of the massive lion and the rugs were too much for the pathetic animal. Her knees folded and she collapsed to the ground. The lion ripped at the mare's back with its powerful claws. Wrestling the horse on her side, its fearsome teeth sank into her neck and it shook her like a toy. The old man watched in horror as his faithful old friend writhed in her death throes. The lion clamped his powerful jaws around the horse's muzzle and snapped her neck. A cry escaped the lips of the man and he immediately regretted it. The lion's head instantly turned in his direction and it fixed its large green eyes on the hiding place. Frozen in terror, the old man listened as its padded feet alighted softly upon the ground, closing in on him. Thinking quickly, he reached down and wrapped his cold fingers around a large rock. Heaving the rock away, he darted for the rocky pass. The lion leaped toward the sound of the rock. The man dashed across the pass and hid in a ditch beyond, gasping for breath. After a while of terrifying silence he got to his feet and, rasping, walked as quickly as he could down the other side of the mountain. In the darkness he tripped over a root and fell heavily. He lay for a moment where he fell, stock still, listening to the lion roar on the other side of the pass. Comforted that the summit lay between them, he continued quickly down. He was overjoyed to find the path again, and he began to run. Careless about the amount of noise he made, he ran until the roaring of the lion died away.

Completely out of breath, he stopped to rest. He put his back against a tree and massaged his bruised, bleeding feet. A great sadness overtook him. He began to weep quietly for his lost companion, and a wave of rage at the lion overwhelmed him. Running his hands through his wispy white beard, he vowed to return with a strong force of men and slay the brute. He took some water from the flask at his side and splashed it over his grimy, tearstained face. Looking nervously around in the darkness, he was reassured by the absence of everything but himself.

He closed his eyes, sighed in relief, and dropped his weary head on his chest. Hours passed as he slumbered exhaustedly. Much later he awakened and slowly came back to consciousness. Remembering all that had happened, he inhaled deeply to calm himself. The smell of warm, rancid breath enveloped him, wafting over his rigid features. Looking up, he gazed into a pair of large, malevolent, green eyes inches from his face.

*Hast thou not seen that unto Allah payeth adoration whosoever is in the heavens and whosoever is in the earth, and the sun, and the moon, and the stars, and the hills, and the trees, and the beasts, and many of mankind, while there are many unto whom the doom is justly due. He whom Allah scorneth there is none to give him honor. Lo! Allah doeth what he will.*

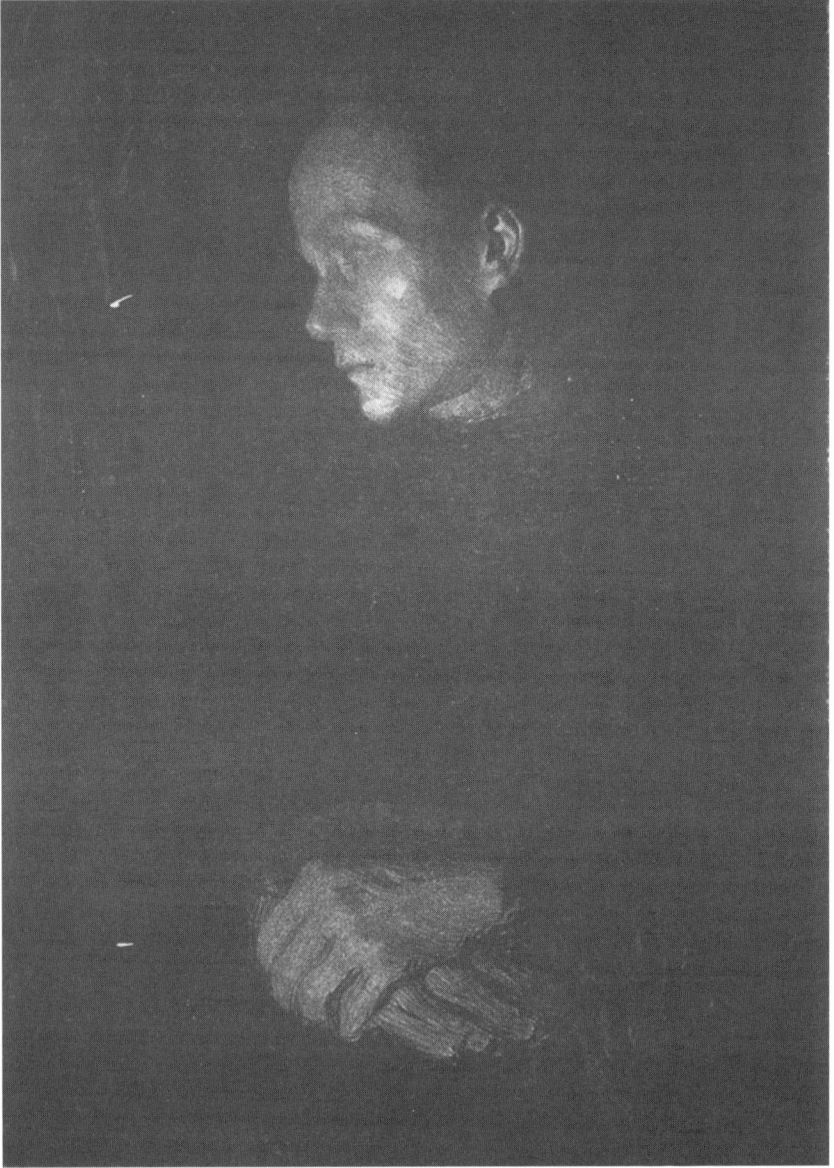

Käthe Kollwitz (German, 1867-1945)
*Working Woman in Profile Facing Left (Arbeiterfrau im*
*Profil nach links)*, 1903
Lithograph on Japanese paper, 16$^7/8$ x 11$^7/8$ inches (image)
Museum Purchase with Curriculum Support Funds, 1997.6.2

# killing frost

*Catherine W. Glover*

he sands while indian summer stretches,
smoothing the bird's eye maple chair
through corn-ripe afternoons—
his design to soothe a fretful infant
into peaceful midnight slumber.

he offers the gift when autumn's shroud
mists fields and muffles bird-song,
a herald to the killing frost
that creeps through uncaulked crevices,
edging panes with icy lace,
webbing winter's sterile beauty.

in january's frozen, fading sunset,
rocker rungs moan and whimper.
she waits, breathless,
but will and wanting
do not shake out the empty stillness
folded in the corner cradle.

leaning on his hand-hewn door,
framed in lengths of evening shadow,
his heart paces
the faint rhythm of her
whispering inhalations.

Second Place, Poetry, Grades 9-12

# Shadow Play

*Jocelyn Spaar*
*Charlottesville High School*

Hands that now hang
like a heavy knot

as a child once spliced
the lamp's glow into shapes

of rabbit ear, dog
face, witch's hat,

knight's spear—
bedroom game

whose only burden
was the loss of light,

and not this hopeless weight,
this endless night.

Kai Ch'i (1773-1828)
Chinese, Ch'ing
dynasty, 1644-1911
Lady in Her Study
with Attendants, 1821
Hanging Scroll, ink and
color on paper, 38 x 17
inches
Collection of the
University of Michigan
Museum of Art. On
view in *The Orchid
Pavilion Gathering:
Chinese Paintings from
the University of
Michigan Art Museum*

# A Profile of I

*Josephine Blount*
*Tandem Friends School*

> I am not I
> I am the emperor's daughter
>
> I am not myself.
> I am the sculpted filling inside of the mold
>
> I am not strong,
> I am the beautiful and delicate cherry blossom
>
> I am not a peasant,
> I am the jade, robed in layers of the finest silk embroidery
>
> I am not an achiever,
> I am spoon-fed by the imperial court
>
> I am not rounded,
> I am dainty and petite and sized to the precise measurements
>
> I am not in love,
> I am betrothed to the man I have never laid eyes on
>
> Who are you?
> For I deceive myself
>
> I am not I
> I am

**Charles Meryon (French, 1821-1868)**
*Le Pont-au-Change,* 1854
Etching with drypoint, 6 1/8 x 13 3/16
inches (plate)
Museum Purchase with Curriculum Support
Funds, 1992.16.2

# Man in Water

*Zoë Ackerman*
*Village School*

Who disposed of me, I cannot tell
Here I am royalty in my own moat!
Attention drifts upward
Where a balloon lies
I feel desperate,
Distant from solid ground
The water is pulling me down
I start to sink,
I am starting to give up
On hope,
And on having a place in
The world.
If only I were up there,
Breathing freely,
Airborne and safe,
Up there in that balloon
But I have no power over what's to
come.

# Man in Balloon

The constant wind blows
My balloon this way and that.
I feel humiliated,
Many stare and point with glee
As my balloon slowly loses air.
I'm soon to plunge
Down, deep into the depths
Of a moat, and will have
No chance to live.

A bit of flailing in the water below me
Catches my eye.
I wish to be down there,
Near solid ground
And not relying on a bag of helium,
Down there near solid ground,
But I have no power over what's to
come.

Second Place, Prose, Grades 3-5

# Robert's Dream
*Joshua Scharf*
*Venable Elementary School*

Back in an old, old town on the river in Massachusetts lived a young man named Robert Potter. He was the governor's son. Robert liked to look down from the high windows in the castle and see stone bridges and glistening water. He would imagine flying on the clouds looking down over his kingdom as if he were a king. When he was not imagining floating in the air, he was figuring out how things like balloons can rise through the air so quickly.

Robert figured out that heat could make his balloons rise in the air. He got out scissors and paper to make a paper man. Then he made a basket out of straw to put him in. Afterwards, he attached strings to the basket and to the balloon. Robert worked hard to figure out how to heat the balloon so it would float without burning. After he finished the model, he pictured himself flying over the river seeing the waving flags from the castle and traveling boats. People in the boats would look up, wishing they were in the air.

One day when Robert was fiddling with his model, his father, the governor, came in and thought he should make a bigger model so people could travel with it. He and his father got the supplies they needed to build the balloon. Once they finished buying what they needed, they went home and began building the balloon. At first, his father was not able to keep up with Robert, but Robert explained how all the parts went together. His father caught on and made a large sturdy basket for someone to stand or sit in. Robert figured out how to make the big balloon and get heat in it without popping it. Late at night, Robert and his father started to put it together with strong rope. When they finished it, they were thrilled.

The next morning Robert and his dad went out early to test the air balloon. They found a spot near the river to fire up their balloon. After climbing in the basket, they untied the rope held by the stake to let the balloon rise. As they lift off the ground, they feel weightless and are grinning more and more as they rise above the river. Robert remembers his dream and it has come true.

Sheng Mao-yeh (active 1594-1640)
Chinese, Ming dynasty, 1368-1644
*The Orchid Pavilion Gathering*, 1621 (detail)
Handscroll, ink and colors on silk, 12³/₈ x 86 inches
Collection of the University of Michigan Museum of Art
On view in the *The Orchid Pavilion Gathering: Chinese Paintings from the University of Michigan Museum of Art*

First Place, Prose, Grades 3-5

# The Orchid Pavilion Gathering

*Emily Berg*
*Meriwether Lewis Elementary School*

There once was a party in China. Most of the people were having picnics. The servants were filling up cups with tea and then putting them on the lily pads to float down the river for people to drink. They were also having bread and butter. Some of the men were making a scroll. A family in the mountains heard the noise from the party. They thought it sounded like fun, so they came back from their picnic in the mountains. Many of the people were talking about their happy times at their cozy homes. Some of the older men and women were telling stories about when they were younger. One of the old women was telling a story about when she was a little girl. Some of the people were talking about building their new houses. They were having so much fun! The women started planning the picnic for next year.

The ducks came swimming up with their ducklings when they heard the commotion and noise from the party. They wanted to see what was going on. The ducks started swimming around the teahouse where the men were making the scroll about the party.

The mothers started to tell their children to lie down and rest. They kept playing and running around. Some of the grownups were even getting tired so they lay down to rest, too. After the people had rested for a while, they got back up and started having fun again. The children started to play with the children who did not rest and the grownups started talking again. They were having so much fun that they did not notice how dark it was getting. In the middle of all the talking and playing someone yelled, "Quiet!" Everyone was quiet except the ducks quacking. When the ducks stopped quacking, it was so quiet you could hear a pin drop. The men said, "Do you realize how dark it is getting?" So the people started to pack up and go home. The party was over.

First Place, Poetry, University/Adult

# The Beautiful Writing

*Don Whitenack*

It is said
one cannot write clearly
what the eye sees clearly.
Words sidle up, and hold back.
Images follow facts
at a safe distance
like ruly servants.
But we must angle for trout
by the trout's reckoning,
so the master of beautiful writing
trims his brush at the pavilion,
while we sport with cups, and
the brook steals coins of light
from Sheng Lake.
Wine, bee drone,
the stream's endless recital
blur the instant
when day tips downward
silvering our beards,
dwindling our stock of
words strong enough
for silk and ink.

It was spring, and we were poets
priests of work and pleasure,
but no matter
how I scrawled and recited,
pressed cup to lip that day,
the wine withheld its layered palate
the festival banners slumped west
and evening gained a grip.

At the pavilion, under
the afternoon's pale robe,
the master's hand waits
to draw our words from shadow,
perfect and still for the ages.

But my words won't last
a day. I am a poet who
doesn't even know
where water comes from,
or where it goes.
Though I have watched bamboo
bow and straighten,
seen servants bend until
their bones touch the earth,
I wonder yet
how a tree wrestles life
from a stone, and how wine,
my best companion,
sometimes fails me.

I withdraw a distance, gaze back
to watch the landscape gain its balance,
and slip my scroll beneath a stone.

**Raymond Parker (American, 1922-1990)**
*Untitled,* 1960
Oil on canvas, 80³/₄ x 69⁷/₈ inches
Presented by Samuel M. Kootz, L.L.B. 1921, in memory
of William C. Seitz (1914-1974), William R. Kenan, Jr.
Professor of Art History, 1970-1974, 1975.1

# A Face from the Crowd

*William Gillespie*
*Jackson P. Burley Middle School*

"Time to try out that new microscope," thought Professor Anaerobe as he entered his lab one Monday morning. He located the shiny new microscope, placed it on his desk, and began to wonder where he could find a specimen. "I'll get some from the staff fountain," he said. "I've always wondered what things lived in that disgusting water." He chuckled, "Even the strongest organism on the planet couldn't survive there."

Meanwhile in the staff fountain, the dastardly trio, the Amoeba Brothers, was plotting their next nasty trick. After using the Streptococcus bacteria as a soccer ball, absorbing the plankton's favorite nitrogen juice, and yelling, "COVER SLIP!" every morning at 1:00 A.M. for a week, the three amoebas wanted to have fun at a higher level. Suddenly, their plotting was interrupted by an enormous, sarcastic voice saying, "Let's see if I can discover any new organisms today!" Then they were sucked up in a dropper and were soon dumped on a cover slip.

The amoebas began to scream, "COVER SLIP!" but then stopped and started to think, and, as they thought, they remembered what the enormous voice had said. An excellent thought popped into their heads. "What if," they all said at once, "we made a huge face using our bodies and fooled the big voice to think that we were a new organism! It wouldn't be able to tell what we really were from its point of view!"

Professor Anaerobe then placed the cover slip under the shiny new microscope and turned it on. The Professor put his eye up to it and twisted the eyepiece, slightly focused it, and then twisted it again. "AUGH!" he screamed, leaping backward as if the lens was scorching hot! In it he had seen an astoundingly inhuman face, with two huge eyes and a gaping mouth just as big! But the weirdest thing was, it wasn't held together by anything! No nucleus, no protoplasm, no cell membrane, nothing! He checked again, just to be sure, but there it was! All of its parts were moving in synchronization, none of the parts was floating away from each other. Professor Anaerobe even saw that when any organism the "face" liked to eat came near, only the "mouth" went up and absorbed it.

Professor Anaerobe was very excited, but he didn't lose control. He didn't know if it was a new organism or not. Just because he hadn't seen anything like it didn't mean it was new, so he called his friend, Professor Escherich, who was an expert at naming organisms, but even he was unable to identify it. Growing more excited by the second, Professor Aneaerobe decided to let everyone in the lab see it, even Professor Giardi, his rival since high school.

Professor Anaerobe proudly hooked his microscope up to the lab television and turned it on. Except for Professor Giardi, everyone oohed and aahed when the "new organism" went up on the screen, especially when the "organism" was intelligent enough to notice they were watching it and to make rude faces at them.

But then something interesting happened. Three of the "good to eat" organisms came on the screen and the Amoeba Brothers faced a dilemma. Should they eat to their nucleus's content or continue fooling everyone and embarrass the Professor on public television. And suddenly a tiebreaker from within told them to do the right thing. It was their vacuoles rumbling, which told them to gorge themselves. When the professors saw the brothers splitting up to catch their meal, they saw that they were not one organism, but three organisms!

Some of the scientists began to grumble, and Professor Giardi shouted, "Ha! You haven't found a new organism. It isn't special at all!"

"But you're wrong," said Professor Escherich. "These organisms are intelligent; they somehow knew we were here and tried to fool us."

"Nonsense! It was just a coincidence," stated Professor Giardi coolly.

"Then how do you explain the rude faces?"

To that, Professor Giardi began to grumble and walked out of the lab.

"We should continue to study these creatures to find out how they know we are here," said Professor Escherich.

"Yes, I agree," said another scientist.

So from that day forward, Professor Anaerobe became famous, the Amoeba Brothers never got a moment's peace, and Professor Giardi continually checked public bathrooms for new organisms unhappily ever after.


Third Place, Prose, University/Adult

# Amoeba, Amoeba, Paramecium

*Marjorie W. Shepherd*

Caught in the eddy, as they were, in the shadow of the riverbank, the three had to confront their dilemma.

"Elenor, honey, I can't take it anymore," Harold pleaded, "Ya gotta make a commitment here. Ya gotta make up your mind."

"How can I tell you anything when I don't know myself? Oh, Harold, I don't want to hurt you, I just don't know if I should be open to other possibilities. I don't know if I can say for sure."

Jake hung back against the bank, flagellating his cilia in Elenor's direction. "Come with me, baby, it's a big world out there, I'll show you a good time," he called.

Harold stretched out before Elenor. "We're two of a kind, Elenor. Two peas in a pod. You and me, we fit. How can you even consider going off with a, a uni-shape? You don't even know if you can...if you and Jake can, you know, *be* together."

"Hey, variety's the spice a life, baby, don't worry about it. He's just jealous of my form," Jake called. Elenor turned in his direction, watching Jake sway.

A little wind jostled them in the water, but not enough to free them from their predicament.

"Listen, Elenor, let me take care of you. I'll wrap myself around you. I'll protect you. You and I could fuse, Elenor. We could become one. Stay with me, honey." Harold was up against her now, his pseudopod shielding the moving water from Elenor's delicate form, stretching to her contour.

"Harold, this is what I'm talking about. This is what I've been trying to tell you all along. You don't know how to give me some breathing space. You smother me, Harold. I need to express my individuality. I need my freedom." At this her voice was rising with agitation.

Harold got quiet. "Remember our dreams, Elenor, you and me, a little pond, some fission and lots of little ones around us? I'm flexible, Elenor, but I can't wait forever."

Jake, aloof up til now, slid across the surface just as easy as you please, and nuzzled his oral groove up against Elenor. He whispered, "Hang on, baby, we'll see the world. You'll move outta this gig and up the evolutionary ladder with me."

A rush of wind and water surprised all three of them. Jake spun and aimed himself downstream like a surfboard on the current. Harold and Elenor, meanwhile, instinctively turned to each other and interwove their folds before the whoosh of water pulled them downstream.

"Together as equals, then," Elenor called out above the roar. They rode, as fingers intertwined, spinning like a carnival ride, resting, finally, in a big open pool, shaded by willows.

"I won't crowd you, Elenor, I'm sorry. You can leave when you want. I just didn't realize."

But before she could speak, before they let go of each other, their bodies rumbled, and with a mighty heave, twin offspring broke away from them. Elenor and Harold twirled and grinned at the sky.

First Place, Prose, University/Adult

# Reaching a Chord

Jennifer Whitenack

It took Frieda a few minutes to realize that it was the painting that had awakened her. She had fumbled with the clock radio in a desperate attempt to capture a few more minutes of sleep, only to realize that the source of the sound was directly in front of her, not to her left where her hand still rested on the snooze button. The heavy canvas, sporting large blotches of teal and purple, was propped against the wall near the open window amid her other flea market treasures—bits of metal and pottery, old eyeglasses, odd gadgets whose usefulness would now be defined by the high-school artists in Frieda's sculpture class. She had added the painting to her purchases on impulse, just because she liked it, rationalizing that it might spark a lively continuation of last Friday's class debate: "But Miss O'Connell," they would sputter, "I could go home and do a painting like that any time I wanted! So why is that *art?*"

Gazing absently at the painting, she wondered who in the neighborhood would be making such noise at 5:30 in the morning. It sounded like a single chord in some minor key, pulsing and insistent. Sighing, she closed her eyes and stretched, vowing that this year she *would* move to the country. The noise stopped. Opening her eyes again, she found that the chord had resumed its irritating rhythm, this time at an increased volume. A chill went through her. Slowly, deliberately, she closed her eyes. Silence. Without opening her eyes she turned her head toward the bathroom door and then, as if to sneak up on the sound, snapped her eyelids up. Nothing. "This is nuts!" she told herself. She glanced nonchalantly toward the painting. As soon as her eye caught a glimpse of teal, the chord re-announced itself. Leaping from the bed, she fled downstairs. "Coffee, that's what I need," she decided.

* * *

Cup in hand, opening the art room door with a well-timed hip thrust, Frieda made it to the counter just as the canvas tote bag slipped from her grasp. The awkward assortment of potential sculpture landed squarely on her sandaled foot. Swearing softly, she gave the bag a kick with her other foot, which both extricated the injured toes and knocked over a cup of purple tempera. Immediately the room filled with rich arpeggios of a tenor sax. Frieda threw a towel over the spill and shook her head in disbelief as it blotted both the paint and the sound. Before she could finish cleaning up, the bell rang and the room filled with energetic chatter. Art I students retrieved paintings begun last week, organized their materials and began to work. Frieda's head throbbed as the noise grew in a steady crescendo: red dots of staccato trumpet, broad blue sweeps of viola, brilliant but piercing piccolo yellow. She found that she couldn't even look in the direction of the student doing the abstract work in shades of orange-oboe and English horn were contesting a lumbering counterpoint, a half step out of tune. She felt a sudden wave of nausea. Raising her hand to get their attention, she shouted over the din: "Class, I must *insist* that you lower your noise level! No one can concentrate when it's this loud!" Thirty stunned faces looked up from their work as if they had been struck, the only sound Frieda's breath coming in ragged gasps. Seeing that she had nothing more to add, the students resumed work. The resulting cacophony surged over Frieda. Fearing that she was about to be sick, she lurched across the hall to the restroom.

Collapsing in the cracked leather chair with a wet paper towel on her face, she concluded that she must have had some sort of breakdown.

She yearned for someone to confide in, but could think of no one. She had always been somewhat disdainful of those acquaintances who felt incomplete without a large circle of friends and family. Frieda had been alone as long as she could remember. She had always been independent, strong. Chills washed over her. Family is who has to take you in when you have nowhere to go, when you go nuts. She began to weep, her face in her hands, nose dripping between her fingers. Other people had photographs and souvenirs of lost loved ones; she didn't even have memories. "You're supposed to be here at times like this! I can't do this by myself!" she sobbed. The echo of her words in the empty room was an accusation. That's why her mother had disappeared—Frieda was too much of a burden, a whining toddler too clingy and helpless to be endured. If she had been a good girl this never would have happened. Shaking, she went to the sink to wash her hands. Afraid of how the neon-pink soap might sound as it oozed between her fingers, she turned and left. She'd tell the office she was sick (if they only knew how sick!) and go home early.

The chord began to throb as soon as she entered the bedroom. She threw herself on the bed and closed her eyes tightly, willing herself to sleep, craving the silence of blindness. Like a child who can't resist wiggling a loose tooth, she took furtive peeks at the painting, testing whether she could control volume and timbre with her eyelids. She turned her back on it, but not for long. It seemed to be waiting for her to turn over and look! listen! "Leave me *alone!*" she wailed, lurching out of bed. She picked the canvas up and slammed it face down on the carpet. The chord, muted, became a hum, rising and falling as Frieda breathed.

*Warm sun on her closed eyelids…the soft humming…arms hold her suspended…swaying gently…her face half-buried in fuzzy teal blue…glint of purple dangling from her mother's neck…the soft humming…heartbeat against her ear*

Frieda opened her eyes. The room was silent.

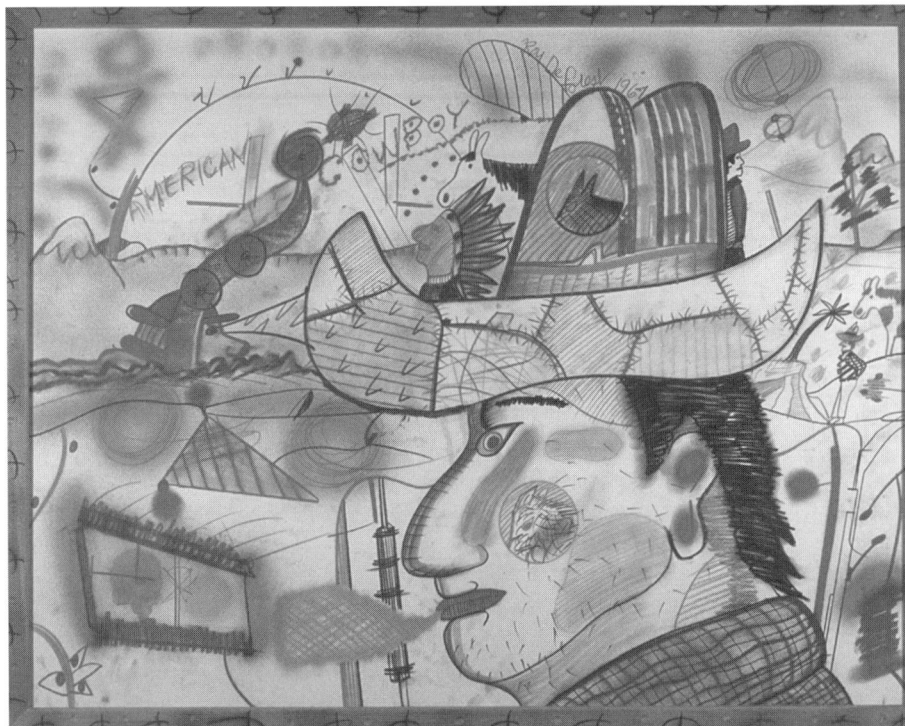

**Roy De Forest (American, born 1930)**
*The American Cowboy,* **1976**
Colored pencil, graphite and pastel on paper,
22¹/₂ x 30 inches
Museum Purchase, 1976.14

# Out with the Real Cowboys

*Emily Moffett*
*Brownsville Elementary School*

He blew orange smoke with the bloke on his hat
his name was Roger,
He got his hat [handmade] for saving his town it was in great danger,
He saved his own life
including his wife's
[They did not exactly live happily ever after]
He had some burnt spots on his face,
He told people they were spots of braveness.
He was an Indian American cowboy you know,
He loved the wild,
he made everything that he had
He made his blankets to sleep on even!
He loved patterns,
He loved to find things
That is why there is a hidden canoe in his hat,
Every once and a while traveling he crossed a lake or two.
One day Roger took his last breaths,
The few friends he had were sad on that day,
even the horses were sad,
his wife was in tears holding his hat.

Third Place, Prose, Grades 9-12

# Smoke Screen

*Alison Kilian*
*Charlottesville High School*

It's the regular pit-stop when driving with dad. I get a candy bar, he gets a fresh pack of cigarettes, or "ciggies," as he affectionately calls them. Waiting for my dad to make his oh-so-important cigarette brand choice, I peer over his shoulder at the minuscule packages of destruction. The Marlboro Man grins back at me in a sweep-you-off-your-feet kind of way. Bleached white teeth, too bright, glare back at me from beneath crinkly, sparkly eyes. His cowboy hat propped jauntily atop his head, he looks young, strong and rugged. There is no hint of aging here, nor any sign of lung cancer. I stare at him harder. He is a picturesque movie star riding off into the sunset and I can still not find a flaw. My eyes hurt from squinting at the tiny, shiny packaging and I turn my head away. My dad grabs a pack and pays and we exit the store. The bell hanging on the door clamors cheerfully in my ear as we exit.

I am your average daddy's girl. When I was little, it may have been my mom who bandaged up my wounds but it was my dad who took me out for ice cream afterwards and stopped my crying. When I am having a lousy day, my dad can make me laugh in a flash with his stupid antics. One of my favorites when I was younger was the chopsticks-up-the-nose trick. Mom didn't like taking the family out to eat at Asian restaurants. The past few years, some of my dad's antics have lost their humor. He more often embarrasses me or annoys me than makes me laugh. I still love him as much as ever, though. He says he worries about me because I take on too much. He bought me a new sweater last weekend. "You don't wear enough," he complained gruffly. "You'll catch your death of cold." I simply gave him a kiss with the returned remark that he was just an old grandmother. He doesn't know it but I worry about him just as much as he worries about me. He has smoked for over 25 years and he goes to the dentist extra often to keep his teeth clean because of the nicotine. In health class I saw a picture of a lung of a non-smoker and a lung of a smoker—absolutely disgusting. The charcoal scribbles and lines and lumps on the lung made no impression on my dad, though, when I pointed them out to him. "Don't worry!" he laughed and proceeded to cheerfully throw bits of balled up paper at me. I smiled and put my health book away. But while I laugh with him, my prayers for him ride heavenward into the smog on a cloud of yellow, filthy smoke.

Italo Scanga (American, 1932-2001)
*Red Cube and Trees,* 1997
Painted steel, 12 x 12 x 11½ inches
Gift of the artist, 1998.3

First Place, Poetry, Grades 3-5

# Memory

*Sarah Mary Goldfarb*
*Walker Upper Elementary School*

The wise, gay old man sits at the park bench,
His sharp
Unblinking
Green eyes in a trance,
Thoughtfully fixed upon two large trees.
An open sketchbook lies across his lap.
With pencil in hand, he thinks for measures of
Endless, beating time.

In his mind he creates a block
Surrounding the trees
Coming fearfully near to the treetops.
But what color is this block?
Red, he thinks.
He colors slowly.
Such a rich red that plasters around the forest-colored trees.
He thinks once more.

They sit in the block without air.
He erases and creates openings in the cube.
Once more he wisely places his thinking cap upon his head.
He glimpses solemnly at the trees and
Without thinking he creates memories
Not remembered but imagined.

The large trees are a mother and infant
The infant first learning to walk, the mother cooing with joy.
The infant's toothy grin is brighter than a snowflake
Lying on the tip of one's eyelash.
It is a blissful turmoil of the child,
Like tasting wine for the first time.

The tree to the left is a child standing on the bridge,
His hand full of corn for the intricately feathered ducks,
Learning to swim
As the infant learns to walk.

The trees are a husband and wife at a wedding,
Their fingers intertwined, as are their lips,
And the groom remembers the time at the bridge,
His fist full of golden corn to feed to the ducks,
Learning to swim,
As the infant learns to walk.

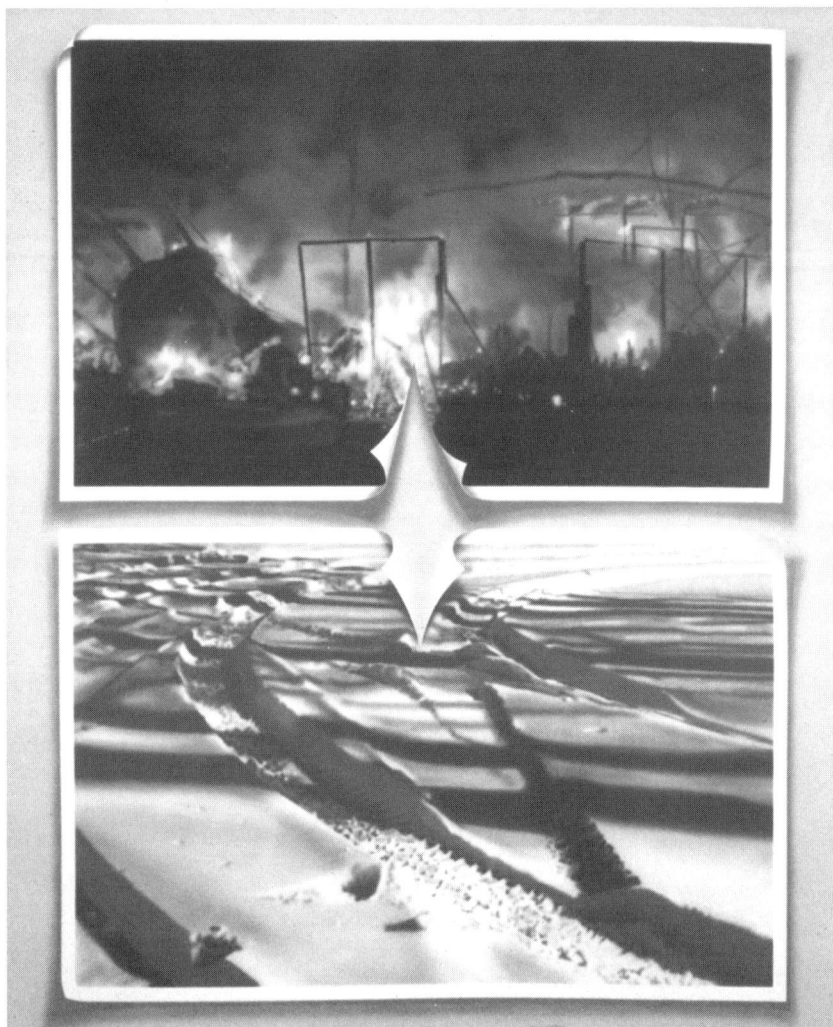

John P. Stewart (American, born 1945)
*The Age of Fire and Ice,* 1975
Acrylic on canvas, 72 x 61 inches
Paul Goodloe McIntire Fund Purchase, 1975.31

Third Place (tie), Poetry, Grades 3-5

# The Town of Fire and Snow
*Candice Roland*
*Virginia L. Murray Elementary School*

Fire and flames.
They are everywhere.
Heat blends into the cool crisp air of a fall morning and overpowers it.
Along with the heat of the flames lingers a tension and rush among the
town's people.
Fire burns and destroys. The wood trembles in the presence of the flames
as it falls to the ground begging for mercy.
Bucket after bucket of cool well water is poured onto the flames yet the
work is all done in vain.
And then…
It is five decades later and signs of the fire are no longer visible.
A soft snow now covers the ground like an icy blanket over the rebuilt
town.
The town sleeps, unaware of the snow atop their roofs.
But not all the town sleeps.
Far away in the woods behind the town,
The snow in the woods has deep tire tracks carved into the perfect white
blanket.
People have been here.
And their tracks are clearly visible.
They seem to ruin the snow.
Take away from its perfection.
Take away from beauty.
Take away from the perfect blanket of an untouched snowfall.
Like the fire destroys the town, the tire tracks destroy the snowfall.

Second Place, Prose, Grades 9-12

# National Treasures
*Stefan Hench*
*Charlottesville High School*

Every spring, after the females gave birth, a herd of caribou stopped on a rare flat piece of tundra in the northern highlands. Here they escaped predators, mosquitoes, and summer heat. When summer ended the caribou headed south again.

War came with the sight of all-terrain vehicles, the sound of engines revving and the smell of diesel. The ATVs left deep tracks in the snow thus far virgin to such a human invention. A bearded one, with stars on his shoulder, got out of his jeep and commented on the defensibility of such a site. Here they could protect their rich oil reserves vital to the conflict. The men mounted turrets and flew a flag over their newfound base. The flag waved alone in the clear air. The soldiers visited the local town during down time and became instant heroes. Their base was founded in winter and the caribou were none the wiser.

The war escalated, and central command sent tanks and planes north, as well as many more troops. The planes needed hangars and the green troops more bunkers. The enemy advanced toward the base but the men only became more resolute. The same flag flew and the hearts of the local patriots swelled with pride. The caribou herded north, but frightened by the sights of war, dispersed with confusion to less suitable nesting grounds. Many of the young were attacked and eaten by predators.

War turned sour and central command decided to all but abandon the effort in the northern theatre. The soldiers left the base with only a brave skeleton crew. The flag flew prouder than ever. The local patriots worshipped their last defenders. The caribou herd migrated south, though too early in the year. Warm weather mosquitoes feasted on caribou weakening many females who had just given birth.

The enemy took the base after a violent battle. The brave soldiers held their position gallantly but inevitably fell to superior arms and numbers. A new flag flew. The northern patriots resented the enemy presence. Women sobbed for the fallen soldiers. Men vowed to carry on their fight and resist conquest. The caribou, though few in number, returned, once again deprived of their sacred ground.

On a clear night, right after vespers, the first bomb, stuck to a tank engine, detonated. Over the next hour, dozens of hand-tied bundles of dynamite exploded, leaving no structure or vehicle intact. The resisters rejoiced in their victory. People saw the snow burning for miles around. Scared by the commotion, the caribou again abandoned their calving ground, frailer and more dispersed than ever.

Two weeks later central command signed an armistice with the enemy. A new border was drawn 300 feet away from the original. The government built a monument over the site of the base for its soldiers who fell for their country. Two resistance leaders received medals. The caribou never returned.

First Place, Poetry, Grades 9-12

## Two visions of torn paper

*Claire Whitenack*
*Albemarle High School*

The grape vines slump in chain-
gang lines, broad shoulders frozen at
the tendriled moment of escape.
Snow smooths the piedmont aisle
of skins and stems where
anxious bees once tunneled toward
sweet purple and asphyxiation.
One truck has carved a road
between the silences of these
museum-rows, the tracks two
tethers toward some other home.
Drawing my first letter's curve,
I know the driver's mind as though
the winter's white were my own page:
To write is to destroy.

In the textbook photograph
the Hindenburg flowers white,
whiter with the phosphorous
explosions of black-hatted
newspapermen, night gathering
dark chins, the static lisp and
stun of radio improvisation
at one with the chew of flames.
You take a burning rib, still
flagged with tatters, as your pen.
Someplace, sirens scream like
desperate kettles over pale
hot roofs, warning thunder or a
leaflet rain. I facing my snow page
am fire-bitten and frost-burned,
certain that all inspiration
ends the same.

Second Place, Prose, University/Adult

# The Reality of Zero

*Adrienne So*

November thirteenth, and for a long time it doesn't occur to me that there's anything strange about the date. As usual, the leaves have fallen without me noticing; they line the sidewalks in sodden golden heaps. I think it was the rain. I was remembering the way the trees were this summer, in their full verdant blush, and I was waiting for the change with mingled dread and anticipation—I hate the cold. But the long weeks of fall drizzle and deluge have kept me inside. Now the trees are naked, and when cars blow by on the roads, the leaves skitter damply in their wake. They are so yellow. It looks like the car's exhaust pipe is shooting flames.

November thirteenth. It's been six months and a day since Daniel and I broke up. We've now been apart for longer than we've been together, and God help me if he wasn't in a dream I had last night. I ran to him and he picked me up like a child, and like a child I glowed and prattled about all the things that had happened to me since he left—all the things that now seemed as though I had been doing them for the sole purpose of having the pleasure of telling him about them. I told him about the way my poetry classes were going and asked if he still read my articles. "Every day, babe," he said. "Every day."

I miss him. But what can I do? The leaves have changed. I have to go on living.

The first time Daniel and I met, we talked about zero. He's a graduate student in mathematics at State; I was taking one of his classes in statistics, and afterwards I asked him what he did. He said he worked on opposites, on the principle that everything has a natural complement that allows it to reach nothing—three and negative three, for example. Five and negative five. It all equals zero.

"But then supposing you have a knot," he said, taking a shoelace out of his pocket and tying a bow with it.

"Who are you, Mary Poppins?" I said. "What else do you keep in there?" "Everything I need and more," he said, grinning and blushing. There was some degree of tension between us at that time. He handed me the string. "Now, what exactly would make the knot equal zero?"

"No idea," I said.

"A backwards knot," he said, slowly sliding the ends till it came undone in my hands. "Voilà, zero. The application of mathematical rules to non-mathematical concepts, and finally we get only a simple string.

But that isn't zero. The string still exists. How do I get rid of the string? I can't. But somehow I've got to try. That's my work. That's what I do."

"Good luck," I said. "As for me, I'd take statistics any day. At least they don't make me pretend to be a magician in a mathematician's costume."

We were lounging on the broken couches in the cramped basement room that served as the graduate student office—three gray cement walls, and one wall of cubbies. Office hours had been over for a good while, and the sky outside was darkening. He leaned over and ran his fingers gently over mine. "What you don't realize," he said, "is that we're all magicians underneath."

I've been thinking about that for a while, how there is nothing that exists without its natural complement—winter and spring, yin and yang, hot and cold. I wondered who had dictated that this mathematical law should be, when even God has his opposite, when even He is subject to the rules of this universe that He created.

Man and woman were meant to move through this world together. I was part of a pattern, and somehow I got shifted out, and it seemed so simple at the time—the idea of opposites. What has a beginning must also have an end.

But now, I can't help but feel as though the months I was with Daniel were a dream, conjured by a man whose life is devoted to the study of magic. An illusionary world, where we could pretend that everything that moves does so hand in hand, coupled mysteriously, inextricably entwined—a world where I could pretend that something this balanced and beautiful could, and would, last forever.

When, of course, things don't work like that. When not everything exists naturally in accompaniment, and not every beginning can have so complete an end.

**Tiziano Aspetti (Italian, 1565-1607)**
*Vulcan,* ca. 1590
Bronze on wood base, 24 inches high
Gift of the Society of Benefactors and Patrons, 1985.41

Third Place, Poetry, Grades 6-8

## Vulcan's Sorrow

*Paul Michel*
*Jackson P. Burley Middle School*

I stoke the fire and do my duty,
Making things of jeweled beauty:
Crowns of gold, and bracelets fine,
Baubles rare of my design.
Some I hope will please my Venus,
Might they spark some love between us?
Armor strong and swords with shields
For warriors on battlefields.
Made by Vulcan, forged from stars,
Yet Venus only longs for Mars.
I, she hates, for lack of beauty,
Still I forge; it is my duty.

**William Wylie (American, born 1957)**
*Untitled* from *Stillwater,* 2000
Gelatin silver print, 20 x 24 inches
Lent by the artist

# Running

*Neil Branch*
*Virginia L. Murray Elementary School*

I am running for my life. I hear my shoes thump on the lake path. I hear my heartbeat. I see a sweaty face in the water's reflection. It is I. The sun's reflection in the water smiles back at me.

It is a cold, gray day. My breath is like a tiny cloud. The crowd far ahead is just a pile of jackets without faces. I see the cameras flash. The other runners are out of sight. It's just me, the wind, the water, and my Nike shoes.

I smell the dew of the early morning. Drops of rain fall from the trees. Ripples in the water show me where a fish has found its breakfast. The wind whips against my face.

My legs are like the pendulum of a clock, swinging back and forth. I am running, leaving behind broken twigs.

I now see a yellow strip in front of me. I hear the rip of the finish line banner. I smell victory. I smell success.

The crowd's clapping is as fast as a hummingbird's wings. The audience throws roses. I then feel the weight of gold around my neck. I am the champion. The man.

# My Grandmother's Eyes

*Beth Foster*
*Jack Jouett Middle School*

"Magic, what do you mean, you know I don't believe in magic."

"Aaah," my grandmother sighed. "Just like you don't believe in ghosts, just like you don't believe in aliens," she turned toward me, looking over the wire rims of her glasses, "and just like you don't believe you'll ever be as old as me." Her great belly shook as she laughed, but then she began another one of her coughing fits as a result of the bronchitis that had imprisoned her lungs. She wiped her mouth, then smiled.

I moved next to my grandmother, studying her, wondering what it would be like to be that old. Her skin hung around her face loosely, as if it were waiting for the perfect moment to drop off. Her hair was thin, and she had dyed it blue, as I had noticed most of her lady friends had done. But the most interesting thing about her was her eyes. Her eyes had a world of their own, never staying the same color. They were a pool blue when she was happy, a dark green when she was mad and a hazel color when she was sad and black when she was indifferent. They often turned a swirling mass of gray, as if she were hiding her innermost thoughts, hiding the wishes and feelings of her brain. And they had a sparkle, a fire that never faded.

She moved next to me. I could smell the cinnamon of her perfume. I nestled next to her, smiling, and preparing for one of my grandmother's famous stories. "This story is about this very lake," she gestured toward the wide open window. The lake was my favorite place in the world, a portrait of beauty and serenity, always there when you needed it most. My tears went into this lake, my flesh and blood was in this lake.

"This lake is made up of the dead, the ones who loved it most. They say their hearts never truly left the place." I watched my grandmother's face, noticing that her eyes had turned a swirling gray, a whirlpool of gray magic. "And every full moon you can go out into the lake at midnight, and stand there, taking in the beauty around you. And, suddenly, your eyes will close. When you open them again, you'll see the spirits around you, the spirits that make up this lake. You may spend the night with them, frolicking and enjoying yourself, but at 7:00, you must leave, and leave that world forever. Once you leave, you'll never be the same, your life will be changed forever."

She smiled down at me and kissed me on the cheek. Her eyes had taken the shade of blue. I began to laugh. "You know that that could never happen. It's impossible."

My grandmother started to laugh.

"And how can you trust an old urban legend?" I began, looking at my grandmother with disbelief.

"An urban legend," she stood up, patting her sagging belly. "It's not an urban legend. In fact, I've experienced it myself."

Several days after she told me the story, my grandmother died, the bronchitis choking her to death. She had called for me, only a few hours before she lay her head to sleep. "Beth," she grabbed my hand, "Remember, always wait for the lake to turn gray. Do not be deceived by the black, brown, blue or green." She stopped there and began coughing again.

Ten years later, I was going up to the lake with my boyfriend. I remember venturing into the house for the first time in ten years. I enjoyed myself, forgetting about my grandmother completely. Until, one morning.

I was searching through my closet. As I shifted a hat to the side, a piece of paper fell on top of me. I looked at the back, the words, "Wait until it's gray," scrawled upon it. I shuddered, dreading what came next. I flipped the paper over and felt my eyes moisten as I saw the front. It was a picture of my grandmother and me, her eyes a whirling gray.

That night I lay in bed, tossing and turning, trying to get to sleep. I stood up to get my book from my dresser. Out of the corner of my eye I saw the moon, a full moon.

"Fine." I pulled on my sweatpants. "If this is what you want me to do, I'll do it." I walked down to the dock, just about to dip my foot in, when I remembered, "Wait until the lake is gray." I sat on the dock, looking up at the moon, humming a song my grandmother had taught me. I watched the lake. It miraculously changed to a green, then a blue, and finally a black. I was ready to go back to bed, my eyelids feeling heavy. Slowly, ever so slowly, the lake turned gray. I dipped my foot in, suddenly feeling a force pulling on my leg. I began to spin, my hair wrapping around me. And then I stopped.

I opened my eyes, and then wider, trying to take in the sights all around me. There were people, animals, floating all around me. I looked into the water, my reflection staring back at me, except I was 60 years older. I saw a young woman, a mirror image of the old me, beckoning for me. I moved towards her and she whispered in my ear, "Welcome grand-daughter. You'll never be as old as me, aye?" I spent the night with her and the lake. I enjoyed her as I never had before. When the sun began to rise, I asked her, "Why did I have to wait until the lake was gray?" She smiled and answered, "Gray is a symbol of love, devotion and willingness to wait. You have truly earned your place here among us," she waved to the gathering crowd, "and among society." I looked in the water, my eyes a whirling gray.

Docent leads a discussion with
students at the University of Virginia
Art Museum in front of a painting by
Raymond Parker, *Untitled*.